Happiness is the Best Revenge

30 days to letting go

*A step by step guide
to letting go of attachment
and heartbreak*

Chuck Spezzano Ph.D.

Illustrations by Brian Davis

Published by Vision Products Limited, Townsend, Poulshot, Devizes, Wiltshire, England SN10 1SD

ISBN 0 9532366 0 9

Other books by the same author:
If It Hurts It Isn't Love
30 Days To Find Your Perfect Mate
30 Days to Getting Along With Absolutely Anyone
The Enlightenment Pack
Awaken The Gods

By Lency Spezzano:
Make Way For Love

Printed in Great Britain by BPC Wheatons Ltd, Exeter.
Illustrations by Brian Davis.

DEDICATION

To my sister, Kathy, for all your love and support.

Contents

Acknowledgements

First of all, I would like to acknowledge the brilliant editing which brought this book to its present state. Thank you Pat Saunders and Brian Mayne. For typing and general support, I want to acknowledge Peggy Chang. Thank you to my students who have taught me so well. For overall love and support, I would like to acknowledge my wife, Lency, and my children, Christopher and J'aime, for their love, support and the grace they are to me.

Thank you all for the wondrous and helpful part you play in my life.

I would also like to acknowledge **A Course in Miracles** for the amount it has influenced my life in an ongoing way, giving me an ever-deepening understanding of psychology and spirituality.

Author's preface

I have lost count of how many times I have had the thought, "I wish I had known this when I was younger." Through individual, relationship, and workshop counselling sessions over the years, I have learned many healing principles. When I or others suffered, I focused on the heart of the problem to find what was causing it and how to get out of it. I learned most of these principles as I suffered through the problems myself, and discovered what worked. Then I used them in my therapeutic practice and found they had universal application. What I learned made all the difference in enabling people to heal themselves quickly. These principles have been tried and tested by years of counselling, and have been found to transcend culture. I have used them freely and effectively in Asia, North America and Europe.

I only wish I had known these principles when I began relationships. It would have saved me a lot of time, trouble and heartache. I have told stories in Japan for many years of Baca Sensei. In Japanese Baca means stupid or foolish and Sensei means teacher. Baca Sensei was the one who had to make all of the mistakes himself, so he could teach the lessons he had learned. I am that one. It's amazing how people can laugh and enjoy my stories of experiences which were pure horror for me as they were occurring.

I have found the principle of letting go to be one of the most crucial principles in life and relationships. It has not been an easy lesson for me. I went to the Olympics in "holding on". I found that my Mediterranean background naturally confused boundaries and made a habit of fusion, which always intensifies any problem.

Having learned these important lessons, I would share them with you. Given a little application, you will find these principles work whether you believe them or not.

Research shows there are typically a number of emotional crises in each person's life which are serious enough to result in hospitalisation. Suffering a loss can be one of the main causes of this. Although this book is written specifically for the loss of a relationship, it can easily be used in situations which include the losses of death, of a job, of possessions, or of other ones. At these times, when it would be so important to have a therapist, counsellor, coach or wise friend to talk to, many people do not have these or cannot afford the help. This book is meant to be that wise friend for those who need it, to assist those who really want – but cannot find or afford – professional help, and to come to the aid of those who are solitary in their pain and who just want to do it for themselves.

Although the problems which arise from not letting go can last a lifetime, my experience is that finding the solution can occur very quickly, sometimes even in an hour or two. I was shocked a half dozen years ago when someone told me of an excellent therapist and author who had cited two to three years as the normal time required to heal a given problem. Some problems may last that long or even longer, but working through the subconscious can greatly accelerate the process.

With willingness and the right circumstances, a problem can be healed in an hour or two. I have seen chronic or major problems – like cancer, alcoholism, an inability to express emotion, screaming nightmares, borderline psychosis or even allergies – clear up in an hour. While this book is designed as a 30-day process, any healing can actually be completed by doing any one of the lessons so well that the rest of the lessons (while still helpful) would actually be superfluous to that particular healing process. If this occurs, I still recommend you go through the rest of the lessons for your education. They will round and smooth out the healing process, and help in healing whatever other problems you might have now or come into in the future.

This book, while not religious, has spiritual principles within it. Over the years I have found that only a fine line can be drawn between higher psychological and spiritual principles. Hopefully, this book is general enough for these principles to fit into your own religious or spiritual framework. Such a framework can be of great assistance in accelerating your healing process.

Life is bigger than any theory. Principles which come from first hand experience over many years are only as good as the artist/author/scientist who attempts to describe them. This book is not meant to contain all there is to know about letting go. It is meant to be a way through whatever challenge you are facing. May it be a step to opening up a new and better present and future for you.

Chuck Spezzano
Hawaii, 1998

DAY 1
Happiness is a choice

Happiness is a choice

Let's face it, there are many reasons to be unhappy. There are enough reasons to last a lifetime. Yet, the experience you have of life depends so much on your attitude and what you finally want and choose. Facing a loss is no different. In the final essay, you choose what will occur and how this will affect your life. "That which does not kill you, makes you stronger." And, thus, ultimately, you choose what any experience will mean to you.

In this loss you have suffered, what is it that you want to occur? What is it you want to be the final result of all this? Do you want it to be the end of you, or the beginning of a whole new level? Do you want your life to stop here, or do you want to learn the lesson involved and become more successful and loving? Do you want your pain to be a monument to the relationship and its ending? Or do you want to receive the love which was given and let happiness become a way of life for you? Will this be a problem you will never get over or will it be the means to springboard to a whole new level in relationships? Do you want to wear a long face the rest of your life, stating: "I am this way, because this person has done this to me? It is at this one's hands that I have been broken?" This is your revenge: to remain emotionally wounded, to state they could not be such a good person if they left you so forlorn. Do you really want to hurt yourself to get revenge? Would not happiness be more effective in every regard?

Exercise

Ask yourself what you are trying to prove by having the letting go process unfold the way it is. When you get your answer, ask yourself what you are proving by that. When you get your answer to this last one, ask yourself what you are proving by it, and so on. Trust what comes into your mind.

What you are trying to prove is just the self concept or identity you are trying to support. It is a compensation, something you are trying to prove, but do not really believe. You could choose happiness instead of what you are trying to prove. Happiness already contains everything you could possibly want. It is important to realise any specific letting go or problem may have several, or even hundreds, of layers. Yet, each choice moves you through one or more layers and forward toward happiness.

'In the final essay, you choose what will occur and how this will affect your life.'

DAY 2
The story of your life

The story of your life

Human beings are story-telling creatures. At the deepest layers of the mind, there is energy and then the mind differentiates into symbols, archetypes, myths and stories. You give your life meaning and, as such, *you* are telling a certain story about your life. And *you* are telling it for a certain *purpose*. This sets up the most primordial patterns of your life. It is more fundamental than, and it also generates, family patterns. Since the major traps in life, relationship and victim patterns, are generated through the family pattern, what our story line is has one of the most generative effects on our life. It is a soul pattern.

Now reflect on how your loss fits into your story. Is it a minor point in your life story? Is it just a step in building to ultimate success? Is it another tragedy in a long, tragic story? Is it the turning point in the story for better or for worse? What happens after this? Is it the climax or just the opening action? This last loss is a chapter in your story. What is that chapter? What will the next chapter be? How are you going to continue telling this story? You get to choose all of this. What do you want in your life? Do you want a happy story, a love story, an adventure story, a discovery story?

The ultimate power you have is to choose and keep choosing a story you really want, as this leads you to it. Choices made continuously in a similar direction become an attitude.

Exercise

If your life was a movie, what would be the title? What would be the story of the movie? Who would you be getting revenge on by this movie?

Take a page and writing in a "stream of consciousness" manner, let the story come out as fast as you can, or use a tape recorder and record it. Examine what's happened and is happening in your life and the story you have written or spoken of as your movie. Where are they similar? How does the pattern of your movie show in your life (your story sets the pattern of your life and experience)? What is your purpose for having this story or having this loss in your story? What story would you choose now?

'The ultimate power
you have is to choose
and keep choosing a
story you really
want ...'

DAY 3
The nature of loss and letting go

The nature of loss and letting go

There are certain principles of letting go which I have found as I have worked with people. The first is that the stages of mourning can take a minute, a year or a lifetime. How long it takes is not dependent on outside circumstances. How long it takes, how fast or how slow the process goes, depends on you. It is your right to decide how long the mourning process will take as it is your experience and your loss. I have known people who decided to complete the mourning process in a minute. This was a beautiful and courageous minute and, at the end of it, they were ready to go on with their lives having integrated the experience of the relationship. I have also seen people who refuse to let go, who rail against the present and hate the future wanting only to go back to the way it was. Angry at life, at the one who left them and ultimately at themselves, they are closed off to life and to what it presently offers them. If you refuse to let go, you will take on one of these self-defeating roles: dependence, independence, or the untrue helper.

Letting go can take months or even years. During this time, you feel depressed, enervated, melancholic, sad and not your usual attractive self. Until you let go, in your mind you are continuing in relationship with your ex-partner, and so have no openness to anyone else. Sometimes, out of anger or pain, you slam the door to relationships, and no one seems to appear until you realise what you have done, and decide to open it again.

The most powerful principle I have found about letting go is this: when you let go, something much better comes to take the place of what was lost. This principle extends to people and situations. It certainly seems paradoxical. When the attachment or fantasy has been let go, there is now an empti-ness which can be filled. There is room for new life. Nature abhors a vacuum. When you let go, it allows you to put things in proper perspective, so you can begin again by living in the present.

Exercises

1   *Today spend about 10 minutes reflecting on the principle that when you let go something better comes to take its place. From time to time throughout the day, consider this especially in terms of your present situation.*

2   *Today, go through memorabilia of the relationship ... papers, clothes, gifts, pictures or whatever. Put these in order. Throw away what needs to be thrown away, and put away anything which needs to be put away, in order to allow you to put things in their present perspective. As you clean up and clean out, experience your emotions. This releases the past and helps you to come into the present.*

'When you let go, something much better comes to take the place of what was lost.'

DAY 4
The stages of letting go

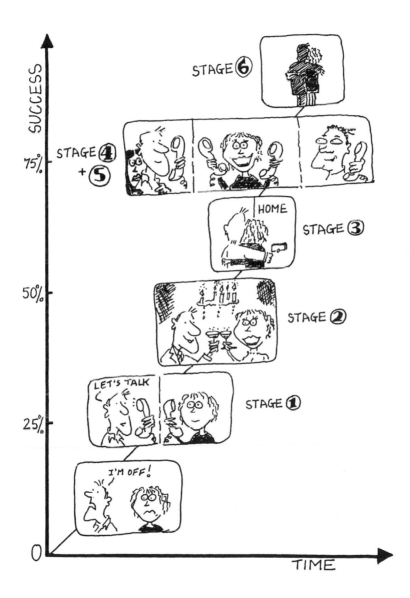

The stages of letting go

There are identifiable stages one goes through in letting go. You can use these stages to recognise where you are, and to prepare for the next step. You are having to let go. This shows that you are working through dependency and neediness. It is most important that you are honest with yourself or your denial will cause you pain.

There are some principles which are especially helpful such as: "Do not call them." This is a situation where your neediness will try to take from them even under the guise of giving. Phone vampirism will hurt your case and lower your attractiveness. You will know when you have succeeded in letting go in the first stage when they have called you. If you have abused the phone, they will not call until the second stage.

When they call, you have reached the first of many stages. Stay as connected and detached as possible. Enjoy the call, but that is all. If you pass this test, you will be invited out to a public place. If you do OK there, they will talk of going out or calling again. They will actually follow through on this if you are unattached to it happening.

When you graduate to the second stage, going out to a public place, you will be tested once again. Again, the key is to enjoy yourself, stay unattached but connected. Your stock rises as this occurs. If you pass the test you are in stage three, and are invited home. If you do OK, there will be more plans to go out and, depending on how well you do, there will be specific, general, or nebulous plans. If you do not do so well, they will promise to call. If you do poorly, you will crash and burn and have to start over, just as you did if you flunked the phone test. Make nothing out of going home with them and enjoy yourself. Stay unattached and that could become a regular thing in stage four. The typical test at stage four is if they have another partner, but want to date you as well. You have almost succeeded. Do not stop letting go now. If you agree, you will be caught in a triangle relationship, a great trap to stop intimacy and love. If you keep letting go, either they or a true partner will now come in at stage five. If you have to make a choice between two people, do not do it. It is a trap. Choose the truth, the next step. Continue to let go of both. Your true partner will join you at the next step with the qualities of both and you will know stage six, True Love.

Exercise

Make a graph of all the stages and where you are in the stages. Study where you are in the stages. Commit to success at the stage you are in, and also for the following stages.

'It is most important that you are honest with yourself or your denial will cause you pain.'

DAY 5

The difference between love and need – if it hurts, it isn't love!

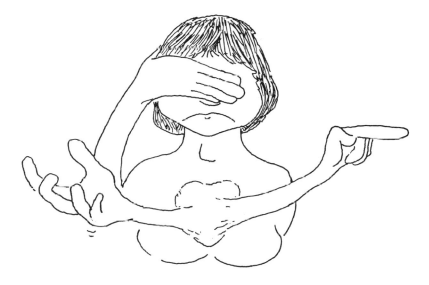

The difference between love and need – if it hurts, it isn't love!

Most of us, when we lose someone and go into a place of suffering, use our suffering as a measure of our love. But this simply is not true. Love does not hurt, need does.

We all have needs, at least this side of enlightenment. Our level of maturity is actually the level by which we handle our needs. Immature forms of handling needs include anger, hurt, emotional blackmail, revenge, indulgence, addiction, complaining, attack, withdrawal, dependence, independence, enabling, dissociation, pouting, "vampiring," taking, manipulation, coercion, control, holding on, power struggle, competition, deadness, tantrums, glamour (that which calls for attention or of making us special by trying to have more, either positively or negatively, than our fellow human beings). Every loss we let go of adds to our wisdom and maturity. Handling our needs wisely through communication, openness and responsiveness, allows us to keep evolving. Voraciousness, denial, or embarrassment does not allow for growth.

It is important to know that the suffering part of what you are experiencing is not true love but merely needs. This can save you both the glamour of suffering, and the illusion of love. What many times is labelled as love was merely the specialness in a relationship. If it hurts it is your specialness that has suffered. For only your ego can suffer and you need not necessarily feel that way. If there is pain, it merely means that your ex-partner did not live up to the script you assigned to them. They broke rules that you had established for them in the relationship. Letting go of your needs allows you to receive and experience the love and connection that is there.

When you are needy, you try to take but cannot receive. When you feel hurt because your partner seems to be pushing you away for no good reason, it is because you are giving to take. If you are not trying to take, you cannot be pushed away because love and wholeness do not make demands.

Exercise

Today, reflect on your present situation along with the suffering you experienced in your family and in your past relationships. Use this idea of love versus needs to motivate you, to let go as much of your past and present suffering as possible. If the past still seems bad or painful, the pain is not merely in the past but still being carried on in the present. Your letting go can simply and easily free you so that something much better can fill your mind and your life. Today, let go of the needs so love can fill your life.

'It is important to
know that the suffering
part of what you are
experiencing is not true
love but merely needs.'

DAY 6

Do you love the person enough to let them go?

Do you love the person enough
to let them go?

This is a true test of your love. Do you love them enough to let them go? Love is an ever expanding blessing, a forever well-wishing, an extending to the other even when it does not seem to serve you. Do you love them enough to wish the very best for them even if that does not include you? Or would you wish to possess them, hold them hostage against their will? It takes courage and trust to let them go.

Would you hold someone against their desire to be some-place else? To control someone is to have them lose their spirit and attractiveness. Your only forward movement is really to let them go. It is only then that, paradoxically, it is possible that they can return to you. You cannot let them go to bring them back, for the nature of letting go is such that letting go to bring someone back is a form of holding on. It just will not work. Letting go must be made with the purpose of living the truth, which is always living in the present, and not trying to foreordain what the truth is. Only through letting them go is there a possibility of bringing them back, but you must truly let them go as if they will be gone forever from your life.

It may be that the only gift you have left to give your ex-partner is to let them go. Otherwise, your attachment would energetically hold them back while paradoxically pushing them away from you. Simply said, you are using them to hold yourself back. Your ex-partner becomes your best excuse not to go on and make something of your life. But, at the end of your life, what it has become is what you made of it, in spite of the challenges.

For whatever gift this relationship has been in your life, would you use it as a trap now? Would you use this time as a monument to your loss or would you use this time to celebrate the love and gifts you have received for however long the relationship lasted? Your relationship is over. There may or may not be another chapter with them, but this part is over. The only way to tell if your ex-partner is in your future chapters is to let go of this one. Reading a chapter over and over, no matter how good, keeps you from going on to the next chapter. And, if you dictate that this is the end of the book of your life, you make it a rather feeble ending no matter how good it was before.

Exercise

Take a good look today at how much you love your ex-partner. If you love them then set them free. Otherwise, look at how much your needs would want you to enslave them and you in what would be a facsimile of a loving relationship.

'Only through letting
them go is there the
possibility of bringing
them back, but you
must really let them go
as if they will be gone
forever from your life.'

DAY 7
The lesson of a relationship

1

2

The lesson of a relationship

Every relationship has a crucial lesson as its purpose. Long-term relationships may contain a number of these lessons. Learning the lesson leads to an increase of love, confidence, understanding, self-worth and wisdom. Not learning the lesson can lead to painful experiences and valuelessness. Some lessons are so powerful that to fail at them would be similar to failing a shamanic or mastery level test, leading to heartbreak, tragedy, crushing failure or feeling as if you were trapped in hell.

Every lesson we seek to learn in a relationship is a lesson of maturity and love. A dark lesson, such as "the opposite sex cannot be trusted", is in truth an unlearned, or only partially learned, lesson.

The lessons you do not learn in your early relationships with parents and siblings, and subsequent relationships, show up again and again until they are learned. If you have not learned a lesson you have faced time after time, it has a way of turning into a trial. Think of some of the trials you have gone through in your life. They were merely lessons which have become chronic.

Many of the unlearned lessons in this past relationship will be completed in the letting go process. As you give yourself to letting go, the lessons which are finally completed will help you be open and happy now.

One of easiest ways to learn a lesson or heal a problem is to give the gift to the person you were called to give the gift to.

Exercise

What was the main lesson you were looking to learn in this relationship?

On the scale of 100 per cent, what percentage would you say you learned it?

What were the other lessons you were looking to learn in this relationship? What percentage would you say you learned them?

Knowing what you know now, how would you have done it differently to learn these lessons?

What was the gift you came to give your ex-partner? Imagine yourself opening your heart and mind at a whole new level and that you are pouring this gift out to them.

DAY 8
Saying yes to life

Saying yes to life

In the face of a great loss, the disappointment is often so strong that we withdraw from life, even to the point of killing the self or personality that was in charge of our mind. When this occurs, the mind is so prolific that a new self will come to take its place. However, we are weakened by this and are much more disassociated from ourselves. This means our ability to succeed, receive and enjoy ourselves is greatly lessened.

When we have been battered by loss, we choose to withdraw. This withdrawal leads to a loss of contact and joy. It becomes unworthiness, guilt and depression. The extent of our withdrawal becomes the extent of our fear. On the other hand the extent to which we are truly connected and bonded is the strength of our confidence. Each step forward builds confidence. If we do not let go, we limp through life as a shadow of our former self.

Saying yes to life is the willingness for life to unfold, and an invitation for the next step to begin. Taking the next step is not so much a literal striding forward as it is a willingness for life in its next phase to come to us. When there is this willingness, life seems to change significantly around us, typically within a two-week period. The next step in life is always better! Even though we do not know what it is, our willingness brings the next step.

Exercise

In this situation, the resolution to a whole new level or chapter in your life simply awaits a sincere and heartfelt "yes" to the next step, your willingness to step toward life and love rather than death.

List the three major heartbreaks you have had in your life. Ask yourself intuitively, on a scale of 1 to 100, how much of the problem you have left unresolved. The percentage you have not resolved, reflects the loss or need still inside you, a place of withdrawal and continued pain. You can choose once again. You can say yes to life in these situations, and by doing so have new aspects of life which have only been waiting for your invitation to come to you.

'Saying yes to life is the willingness for life to unfold, and an invitation for the next step to begin.'

DAY 9
Taking the first step

Taking the first step

Taking the first step in the letting go process can sometimes be the hardest, and things typically get easier after this point. It is usual for you to find you have your own favourite style in letting go. Even though a general style might also serve you well, you may find other exercises and methods also helpful. Pain comes up layer by layer and, after a state of peace, you may find an even greater layer of pain. Sometimes, after you have had a breakthrough, instead of the situation being better, it seems worse. When it seems like things are getting worse, they are actually getting better, because you are going into deeper layers of pain. This can come up on anniversaries of really big losses, so six months, one year, two years, five or ten years later, a new layer might emerge. When you are in a bad mood, but have no sense of what it is, trust your inner healing mechanism for timing. Ask yourself, intuitively, what the pain in your life is which has to do with this bad feeling. It may be that, in every new stage of evolution you reach, one of the painful events of your life is coming up to be healed at different layers.

Often, layers and layers of pain come up, not so much because there is that much pain, but because the person involved is afraid to suffer anything new, being more willing to trust the devil they know than the one they do not. In this fear to trust and move forward in their life, they use this 'manufactured' pain as a means to keep themselves back. It is important to recognise when you have such a refusal going on, as a result of fear of going on with life. No amount of therapy or other methods will seem to work, because you are manufacturing pain as fast as the therapy or letting go process may be trying to clear it. This is time to resolve and commit yourself to take the first step. If you find yourself malingering, it is important to set goals of letting go for yourself. If you are having a bad day, set very small goals for yourself. You will be energised and moved forward every time you complete a goal.

Exercises

1   *Every grievance stops you by anger, withdrawal and subconscious guilt. And every loss is connected with a grievance, for sadness and guilt go hand in hand. So say out loud: 'I forgive you [name of person] for [grievance]. I will not use this to hold myself back.'*

Do this over and over again with specific grievances. You may find that other people also come to mind in order to be forgiven, eg. past relationships, parents, etc. Do this exercise with them also.

(Exercises continue on next page)

2   *Clean out the paraphernalia of the relationship which now no longer fits your life. Clean out your purse, briefcase, drawers, pantries, closet, etc. You can do this with someone else's help, if that makes it easier.*

3   *Make a list of incomplete projects. Let go of those which no longer fit your life. Reset goals for the ones which do fit.*

DAY 10
The courage to have the feeling change

The courage to have the feeling change

Your loss is a significant opportunity for stepping forward. Many people, in a mourning situation, do not want to change or to move because they are frightened to have the intense love they feel for the one they have lost change in any way. But it is important to recognise some principles which will help you move forward. Again, most of the deep, intense, passionate love is more of a need/desire/urgency experience than a love experience. Love is, for the most part, a steadily radiating, and ever deepening, experience. Secondly, if there was ever any hope for the relationship, or at least to spend some time with your partner again, the only way this can succeed is for these intense feelings to change. Even the sad feelings must change to ones of unattached brightness and expectancy towards life, not expectancy towards your ex-partner. You may also find you are not attached so much to the person of this ex-partner as you are to the feelings about the person, including the sadness.

I have had numerous clients who broke up with their partners and were deep in mourning. They had seemingly forgotten the fact that they did the breaking up themselves, or that it had been mutual. A few weeks after the break-up, they began to change the history of the break-up in their mind, and started to feel abandoned by their partner.

Once again, some courage on your part is called for, so the feelings can run their cycle and finally come to one of peace. As peace and a feeling of detachment are reached (such as, "it's OK if it works and OK if it does not, although I prefer it to work") then life will prepare itself to serve you up your next lesson in relationships. As a new relationship, or the next chapter in this relationship, comes about, new feelings of romance and intensity naturally begin again.

Exercise

Use your present emotions as fuel for this exercise. It does not matter how positive, negative, tender or dead they seem to be. Make a work of art which symbolises the relationship. This could be in the form a poem, collage, song, painting, story, drawing, dance or whatever form you choose. When you have finished it, burn it, keeping only a photograph or copy if you want. If it is a real work of art, sell it or give it away rather than burn it. This exercise can be repeated as you feel inspired.

'Your loss is a
significant opportunity
for stepping forward.'

DAY 11
The purpose and length of the relationship

The purpose and length of the relationship

Every relationship has a purpose. Part of that purpose will be the lessons which were to be learned in the relationship. The main purpose of every relationship is happiness; making you and your partner happy. When you are not happy in a relationship, the purpose becomes healing. Every block between you and total enlightenment will come up between you and your partner. As you heal , more things come up to be healed. As you both grow in confidence, you naturally become much more intimate, successful and happier, and able to deal with greater problems in an ever-increasing creativity with your partner.

Besides healing the blocks in your mind, there seems to be a special function each relationship can fill, which is its own function or contribution in the world. Also, it seems that within each relationship there is the power to save the world. Relationships are a continuum of healing and happiness. By the evolution which takes place in a relationship, more and more people around are helped and inspired. By the healing which happens between two people, and the love which grows, new answers can come into being. Love is one of the best sparks of creativity. The further you progress in your own healing, the more you are shown the way for your own natural leadership.

Every relationship on this earthly plane has an ending. The relationship may last for only a short time or for a lifetime. Usually lifetime relationships are ones where we have a suitable learning partner to learn lesson after lesson together. Then, there are those relationships which last for a shorter duration, perhaps to learn a certain lesson, or to enjoy a certain time together. In addition to these there are the seemingly chance and brief encounters, which are also purposeful, if short-lived.

Sometimes the purpose in relationships is only to get you in touch with a hidden block or conflict. At other times, one relationship may be there just to get you ready for another lifetime relationship just ahead.

Exercise

Ask yourself intuitively what the purpose of your relationship was and trust whatever seems to pop into your head.

If nothing seems to pop in, reflect further on the possibilities throughout the day.

Ask your Higher Mind today to show you what the purpose of your relationship was, and to help in the easy completion of any unfinished purpose from it.

'Every relationship on this earthly plane has an ending. The relationship may last for only a short time or for a lifetime.'

DAY 12
The fire of sacrifice

1

2

The fire of sacrifice

While every sacrifice is a place of inauthenticity, a place of not receiving for fear of intimacy, and fear of the next step, there are times in our lives when we present ourselves a very painful circumstances or a seemingly tragic situation. The purpose of this circumstance is to reach a whole new level of consciousness and birth. If we do not understand this, as an opportunity to advance to the new level of joy and creativity, we can feel as if our life has ended. The new birth is achieved by letting go of every attachment and by welcoming the new beginning as if it were already accomplished. When that which was lost is freely given back to life, the loss is no longer experienced as a sacrifice, and your new life is about to begin.

To have reached this place, you will most likely have to let go of the person, the relationship you had together, your life as it was, and your dreams for how it could have been. Having done this, you see and feel yourself in a higher place of consciousness, more open to life and grace. You are ready to embrace this new chapter in your life, thankful for what was and thankful for what is.

Exercise

Today, take a new attitude towards pain. Use the mourning – letting go process – as one which heals, raises up, blesses, frees and begins life anew. Your choice and willingness allows present and past pain to be moved through, naturally, easily and quickly, so you can evolve. While you are in the labour of letting go, make the choice to move as gracefully as possible, so that what seemed like the end of your life will only be the end of a chapter, and the movement to a higher, better, chapter of love, life and joy.

'When that which was lost is freely given back to life, the loss is no longer experienced as a sacrifice, and your new life is about to begin.'

DAY 13
Saying good-bye

Saying good-bye

It is really helpful to be able to share with an ex-partner and say good-bye, and to have a summary of the relationship put in perspective in your life. It helps to tell a person what the relationship meant to you, although, sometimes, because of death, or the other leaving abruptly, you are not able to have this communication. Again, it is not recommended to call someone who has broken up with you, because under the guise of letting go, you may try to 'vampire' them, but because of your denial you will have no realisation as to why the call did not work. If your ex-partner has not contacted you then it is best to do this part of the letting go on your own. Over two decades ago, in response to a friend who had lost her beloved through cancer, I had an inspiration which has helped many people in the termination process. If you are not in direct communication with your ex-partner, you may wish to write a letter or to get into a candlelit bath and speak to them either out loud or in your mind. You may find this easiest to do in a meditative setting with soft music playing in the background.

Exercise

In whatever setting or medium you have chosen to do this exercise, write to your ex-partner, or tell them out loud or in your mind, what you loved and appreciated about them. Often it helps to imagine or feel them present as you say these things to them.

Now share with them what did not work for you, where you are angry or feel incomplete.

Now share with them the best thing about the relationship, or the best thing which happened in it.

Share with them the most painful part of the relationship.

... the funniest thing in it.

... the saddest thing, or biggest loss, you experienced.

... the happiest time in the relationship.

... the thing which they gave you that no one had ever given you before.

... the most beautiful, tender part of the relationship to you.

... the worst part of the relationship to you.

... what gift they inspired, or called out, of you which you did not know was in you.

... what lesson you learned with them.

... what old pain or fear you got to heal through the relationship.

... imagine you were writer, director and star in the relationship. What scene in the relationship would you rewrite to be better and how would you rewrite it.

What was the part you regretted or felt guiltiest about?

What was the hardest thing you helped them through and that they helped you through?

What is it you would like to thank them for, and thank God for them about?

DAY 14
The truth

The truth

In studying the dynamics of healing principles, I discovered a number of interesting aspects. One was that the dynamics of truth, commitment, freedom and ease are basically the same in their healing effects. Another was all of them lead to partnership. When Jesus said, "The truth shall set you free", he was stating the natural connection between these two healing principles. Likewise with the connection between truth and ease; the extent of the truth is the extent to which things go easily. Given the results of your relationship, either the relationship was not true, or the way in which you lived it was not. Given the principle of truth, difficulty in the letting go process is simply not the truth. In truth, letting go can be one of the easiest healing methods there is, you simply stop holding on. When this occurs the letting go brings about a flow of poignancy.

Having truth in your life gives you a sense of direction and puts things in their natural perspective. Holding on gives you pain – or gives you attachment, which is future pain. Truth also brings to you the freedom you have been missing. Truth is not lonely. It is what leads to partnership. It allows the giving of yourself and the receiving of others which results from commitment in your life. The break-up you have been going through is trying to signal you that you have not been true to yourself or to your life in some way. Otherwise you would not have this kind of pain. Emotional pain is really just a way of letting you know when something is not the ultimate truth. Also, this pain, at the very least, speaks of self-deception, of areas where you mistook your attachment for love. Any attachment is a form of self-deception. It is the thought that something outside you can make you happy. But the truth frees you, just as letting go leads you towards the truth. Pain is just a way of knowing there is still some way to go, still a lesson to be learned for the truth to be known.

Exercise

Today, keep asking for the truth to be given you. What is the truth for your life right now? Are you acting in a truthful way?

Examine the relationship for areas of dishonesty and self-deception. If it was dishonest, typically it reflects areas of self-deception in yourself. Let go of anything you still may be holding on to in this regard.

(Exercise continues on next page)

Are how things are, the truth for you? If not, how do you want to change?

Ask for the truth to be shown to you today. Listen for the truth. Feel and sense what the truth is today. If you ask for the truth today, anything can be a vehicle of the truth for you ... something someone says, something from a book, a TV program, a thought, a dream or a symbol. Just ask for the truth and ask that when it comes you will recognise it as your message. Be aware today and the truth shall set you free!

DAY 15
Letting go of guilt

Letting go of guilt

Any time we withdraw, any time we feel emotional pain of any kind, any time we feel bad, there is an accompanying feeling of guilt. Guilt, basically, is feeling bad about the past. The bad feeling of our past suggests the future will be the same. Thus fear, which is trying to live in the future, comes out of the unmourned past, the unfinished business of the past. Guilt is a mistake turned into a monument. It keeps us nailed to the past, rather than learning its lessons and moving forward. Guilt is a trap which keeps us punishing ourselves. "Don't bother punishing me, God, I'm doing it myself!" Having punished ourselves or having created loss and punishment to pay off our guilt, we then feel bad/guilty about being victimised, and the cycle continues. At the bottom line, guilt is a psychologically destructive trap we use as a way of not facing the next step. Guilt is not the ultimate truth. All that is true about guilt is that we experience it and have layer upon layer of it buried within us. When a situation is fully understood, guilt disappears.

Feeling bad about, and regretting, what happened in our relationship is a way of holding on. Any unfinished business in the relationship, any sadness, anger, etc. goes hand in hand with guilt. Guilt is a form of arrogance, a dark glamour which exaggerates our importance, keeps us stuck, and denies the responsibility (or response-ability of every co-created event). We are all doing the best we can, given inner and outer pressures, and yet, paradoxically, we can all do better. We have all made big mistakes in what we thought was best. 'Unearthing' through feelings is what ultimately corrects guilt by allowing us the possibility of a new level of understanding which frees us from the vicious cycle of loss/need/fear.

Guilt from past losses sets up present losses and self destructive patterns. These are the psychological patterns we carry from childhood. To forgive ourselves and let go of the guilt is one way of freeing ourselves from these patterns which promote failure, sacrifice and valuelessness. Remember, your guilt keeps you withdrawn and unattractive, and punishes everyone you love by your absence.

Exercise

Outline three events from the past you still feel guilty about. Ask yourself how you are punishing yourself for this guilt.

Now ask yourself what you feel bad, guilty or a failure about in regards to your last relationship. Ask how you are punishing yourself for these feelings.

(Exercise continues on next page)

Ask to see the truth of your and everyone's innocence. Let go of the guilt. You can do this on your own. Ask your Higher Mind to let go of any remaining guilt, thus bringing you understanding and peace instead.

DAY 16
The refusal to let go

The refusal to let go

Many times a refusal to let go is an indication more than one person is being held onto. This could mean a dream or self concept was shattered, or that a fusion or heartbreak was involved, which reflected the same experiences from childhood.

The refusal to let go is malingering which uses the present loss as an excuse not to move forward. This pattern is at the heart of our conspiracy against our true self, our purpose and our greatness. It is using victimisation as an excuse not to move forward in a specific area in which we have become frightened to proceed. Often this is because we could not possibly figure out what the next step is, or how we could accomplish it. But that is not our job. Our job is willingness. With willingness we are moved forward, and the next step comes to us. We do not have to figure it out. Figuring it out would only delay us, being just another form of resistance and control. We are moved forward and fear is transcended by our willingness. Also, by our willingness, what is accomplished is accomplished through us, but not by us. Whenever we try to do it ourselves, we do it with graceless difficulty. With the attitude of "not by us, but through us", we just need to show up; what we need to say or do will be given us. This allows for grace, and bypasses control, which is generated by fear, old heartbreak and authority conflict. Our performance anxiety, our perfectionism, our feelings of inadequacy, our lack of trust which leads to control and fear, any competitiveness or sense of failure – which the deadness in our life hides – are all answered and transcended by letting things be done through, rather than by us. The more we try to do everything, the more stress, difficulty and unnecessary hard work is created. And the more we try to do things, the more fear we feel about the future and the more guilt or failure we feel about the past.

The way your relationship turned out shows it was obviously something you were trying to do yourself. Every time you feel badly, it is a signal of something you were trying to do. You can use the times you feel some kind of emotional pain as an opportunity to let go of a whole pattern of 'doing'. This allows for whatever is to be done, to happen in an inspired way.

Exercise

Today, be willing to change or have changed for you any area you have been holding onto in your last relationship.

Make a list of what you are trying to 'do' in your life. Items on this list will reflect areas of guilt, pain, failure, fear, insecurity, scarcity, difficulty and luck of success. 'Doingness' blocks inspiration, creativity, ease, freedom and vision. Be willing to study the effects of letting this 'doing' go. Everything can be accomplished gracefully through, not by, you.

'We are moved forward and fear is transcended by our willingness.'

DAY 17

Forgiveness as a form of letting go

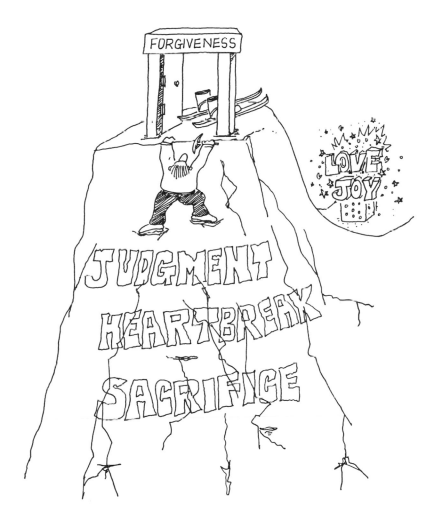

Forgiveness as a form of letting go

Forgiveness finishes unfinished business. It ties up loose ends and allows for a new beginning. Forgiveness releases the other as it releases you. It frees you from the stuckness which grievance generated. It also frees you from the stuckness of subconscious guilt which every grievance hides. There is virtually no one with whom we do not harbour some grievance. In my work, I have found the amount of grievance, either apparent or subconscious, is the amount of pain, lack of success and scarcity in any area.

As you forgive your ex-partner and yourself, you will find a new day dawning for yourself, the beginning of a new chapter in your life. Each grievance you release from others allows you to progress.

Forgiveness seems to be the hardest lesson for human beings to learn. To accept forgiveness, it is necessary for us to let go of our righteousness. Our righteousness allows and justifies our being angry, ostensibly to defend ourselves, but actually to allow us to do whatever we want. But this does not allow the hidden guilt present under every grievance to be released. At the deepest level of the subconscious, we have collusion in a partner's behaviour. Awareness of this victimisation as a collusion can help heal by allowing us to bring up and face buried feelings about it. On the other hand it can be used merely to justify our doing something we wanted to do all along, but otherwise would not have allowed ourselves to do, eg. if a partner has an affair, it is used to justify having an affair or getting a divorce, which was likely something the other partner subconsciously wanted to do. To use this situation to let old pain and un-finished business surface in the present can turn this situation from heartbreak to healing, especially once we realise why we would co-create such an event.

Forgiveness sets things straight and opens the door to living life fully. It opens once again to the good things life has to offer. Forgiveness offers a lot, mostly yourself, given back to you, freed and successful, no longer buried in conscious grievances and subconscious guilt.

Your grievances lock you in a world which never was. Grievances are subconscious projections where we accuse others of what we are doing, although sometimes hiding, denying and appearing to act opposite to what we are judging. Forgiveness frees us of this pattern and brings us back to the present.

Exercise

Imagine the person you have the grievance with standing in front of you. But now, look beyond their mistakes, beyond their personality and beyond their body – just see, feel, sense or imagine the light that is their spirit inside them. Imagine your light joining with their light.

Ask your Higher Mind to accomplish any forgiveness which may seem beyond you, bringing you the peace and understanding necessary for moving forward.

'As you forgive your ex-partner and your-self, you will find a new day dawning for yourself, the beginning of a new chapter in your life.'

DAY 18
'Burning' emotion as a form of letting go

'Burning' emotion as a form of letting go

There is a simple form of healing, a simple form of letting go. My wife, who recognised, named and refined the method, called it 'burning'. It is an apt name. Given any sort of willingness, this is both simple and effective. You simply feel what you are feeling. As you feel your feelings, which include pain, guilt, emptiness, blackness, deadness, numbness, blocked feelings, things begin to unfold to other typically deeper and worse feelings. But as you have the courage, you feel these feelings and move through them to more neutral and then to joyful feelings. Suppressing emotions disassociates you and makes you independent instead of interdependent. Suppressed emotion automatically becomes stress. When you suppress emotion, the emotion itself becomes lost energy and it takes additional energy to keep the emotion suppressed. This loss of energy can keep you tired and even depressed. The great majority of those I worked with who had catastrophic illness had great caches of buried emotion inside. Releasing this energy does not kill you, but keeping it inside might.

These emotions are layered inside us like tunnels going deeper and deeper inside until we are finally past the painful feelings and are into the joyful feelings. But later, we may stumble on another layer, or another tunnel, of feeling. It is important to know that feeling emotion does have an end and it will not go on forever. An added benefit of burning your emotions is that, as you burn them, you reassociate with your feelings. When you move into deeper layers, you not only reassociate with your feelings, but also with your body, sexuality and spirituality. As you open yourself to feeling, you open yourself to the same extent to receiving and relationship.

After a loss a person feels a glut of feeling. It is a very good time to reconnect with yourself starting with the painful feelings at hand. Simply feel what is there to feel, exaggerating or leaning into the feeling, so as to move forward at an accelerated pace. Any feeling which is less than joyful can be grist for the mill. It just takes the courage to feel and you begin making progress.

Exercise

Today, spend as much time as you can feeling your feelings. In truth, you can burn emotions and do most anything else. So, burning can be a background or undertone to anything else you are doing, such as eating or working. You can even tell yourself you will continue burning in your sleep. Burning is a good basic healing method. Some people find this is their favourite method. Given some willingness and courage, it will move anything. As this method progresses, there seems to be a natural evolution toward more grace and love.

'As you open yourself to feeling, you open yourself to the same extent to receiving and relationship.'

DAY 19
This loss hides a greater loss

This loss hides a greater loss

The greater the loss, the more it hides an older, deeper loss. This old loss was the root which blossomed into the fruit of this present loss. Many times a loss is hard to let go of because it is not just a single incident but a whole pattern. However, because of this, there is also an ability to heal the whole pattern by dealing effectively with the present loss.

What has consistently shown itself while working with the subconscious in therapy, was that traumas in our lives do not just happen but have a precedent. And, the greater the present problem, the greater the original loss.

It seems to take great awareness and maturity to realise everything happens for the best, especially in our own lives where the first tendency towards loss is depression, value-lessness, fear, failure, guilt and sadness. These are the very feelings which have, for the most part, already been buried within us waiting for an opportunity to be finally trans-cended. One of the most surprising things I learned in therapy was that present feelings of pain were most often already present in the subconscious, and the present situation was just the trigger for the flowering of them, with actually very little of the emotion coming from the present situation. If we are totally unaware of the subconscious, we will mourn all of the past and present feelings under the aegis of the present loss. But it takes great awareness and maturity to realise this. One way to realise it is to complete the letting go process. In this, you naturally realise what is past and what is present. And, as you do, the next level of your life begins.

Exercise

In thinking of your present loss, if a previous loss has not already occurred to you, ask yourself intuitively at what age the previous loss may have occurred. Then ask yourself who was present when the loss occurred. Ask yourself what was it that must have occurred in order for you to have created such a pattern of loss. In the original scene, ask yourself what everyone must have been feeling to act the way they did. Typically, there is a core painful feeling everyone shared. It is the same feeling which is now part of your pattern. Now look at everyone in the scene, asking yourself how long they had this pattern, where it began for them and how it showed up in their life, as pain or defence against pain or both.

'There is also an ability to heal the whole pattern by dealing effectively with the present loss.'

DAY 20

This loss hides a place of sacred fire

This loss hides a place of sacred fire

It has already been stated that with any major loss there has been a previous loss or heartbreak so severe that were we to live it again, it would take us to our knees. This is an area of the mind I call Sacred Fire-Pain or Sacred Fire-Purification. It is pain so severe people will go into rage rather than allow themselves to experience it. Or, there is the usual ploy of trying to run away from it, or attacking the person closest to us. (If I am hurting this bad, it must be their fault!) Ultimately, these defences do not work and this pain, rightly seen, signals birth, not death.

What is happening is that two major fragments of our mind, which were fractured in some great, past pain are now coming back together. All the pain which kept them apart is coming up. The dire emotions of Sacred Fire-Pain are heartbreak, jealousy, terror, futility, uselessness, hopelessness, anger/rage/violence, desperation, despair, nothingness, emptiness, loneliness or the feelings of being completely lost and cursed. Again, Sacred Fire-Pain is identifiable because of the degree of pain. You feel knocked to your knees. Awareness is one of the key aspects to get out of such dire pain. As soon as you implement the simple yet profound solution, the pain is transformed. It is that degree of pain which is so distracting and consuming that, at times, even knowing the solution, we are still caught for a time in the pain. The pain actually is a form of purification which, as it is experienced, brings about the integration of healing of a major aspect of the mind. But only those most advanced emotionally and in maturity can stand to do it this way. Most of us find a way to turn away from the pain, leaving ourselves unbirthed, still fragmented, and once again disassociated.

As soon as you realise you are in Sacred Fire-Pain, you need only give through the pain to help someone. It may help to imagine a ring of fire you are stepping through to help someone. You might ask who needs your help, seeing them on the other side of the ring of fire.

Through giving, the pain is transformed. It is transformed to Sacred Fire-Birth or Love, or one of its other forms, such as vision, purpose, creativity, art, healing, a vision level gift, or vision level sexuality, a psychic or Shamanic gift, beauty and love. So, from a place of withdrawal and constriction, we can reach a new level of greatness, confidence and power.

Exercise

Today, with any pain you feel, ask yourself who you are called to give to and how. It may be as simple as sending loving thoughts or blessings. It may be calling or contacting them in some way. Or, it may even be a creative project which would be a gift to many people.

Today, your giving transforms your pain to a new birth of creativity and love.

'Through giving, the
pain is transformed.'

DAY 21
Changing life patterns

Changing life patterns

We all have patterns in our lives of success, or of lack of success and failure. Let us begin to examine these patterns. For the sake of our topic, we will examine patterns in relationships, but again, these can be extrapolated to examine other patterns in your life. First of all, notice what your life has been like: what is it you are always thinking and saying to others about your relationships? From root-like, traumatic and often repressed experiences, we have patterns which branch up and out like trees. Have you ever asked yourself why your relationships never seem to turn out? ... Or why there is never any fire in your sex life, no matter who your partner is? ... Or why you are always abandoned? ... Or why certain things always seem to happen to you?

We will approach your life patterns, not only dealing with your conscious, but with your subconscious mind. First of all, your patterns are there for a reason. They are there to protect you from your fear of losing what you have, to protect you from your fear of the unknown, to block gifts and abilities you are frightened of, to serve as a defence over deeper pain and patterns and, finally, they are there to keep your self-conspiracy in place. Your self-conspiracy is there to block you knowing yourself and your greatness, and to keep you from your purpose. For all of these reasons, a self-defeating pattern is not true. It can be removed. The more courage there is to face the next step, the easier it is. Yet, in the blocks to the vision area of the mind I call the Great Fears, the fear of success racks up a bit stronger than the fear of failure. In longer workshops, when we get down to core life dynamics, the fear of having it all, or the fear of God or of happiness, emerges, strangely enough, as the most primordial.

Today is a good day to choose to let the past or these patterns no longer run you.

Exercise

Make a list of the beliefs and patterns you notice in this break-up and in your relationships, eg:
   Relationships never work out.
   All men are ...
   All women are ...
   Sex is only ...
   I am always abandoned.

(Exercise continues on next page)

For each belief you no longer wish to keep, allowing it to support a self-defeating pattern, say: 'This belief is not the truth. This belief reflects a goal which is keeping me from my purpose. What I now choose to believe is ...'

Pretend you want that pattern. Why do you want it? What purpose does it serve? With it, what don't you have to face that is so scary to you? What does it prove? Who is this pattern getting revenge on? What gift am I afraid of?

DAY 22
Reviewing the nature of revenge

Reviewing the nature of revenge

Revenge does not work. It is an attempt to get back at another for what you think they have done to you. Revenge can be an active attack against the other, or it can be a form of hurting yourself to get back at them. Actually, any problem, consciously or subconsciously, such as illness, failure or accident contains core aspects of revenge. But revenge does not work. If you "live by the sword," you "die by the sword." While revenge is an attempt to make up for or defend against the original hurt, it does not do that. Revenge does not satisfy you. The glee revenge brings is small compensation for your hurt, and it reinforces the pattern, meaning you are left being the victim or the victimiser.

As soon as we move into the subconscious mind, we find other principles which belie the need for revenge. The first one is this: no one can do anything to you which you are not already doing to yourself. So, if you feel someone is breaking your heart, you were already breaking your own heart. If you feel they abused you, it was you who were also abusing yourself. Interestingly enough, when this subconscious piece is healed with yourself, it becomes easy to forgive and let go of painful situations.

Revenge misses the point. It makes life about some problem rather than about ourselves. At this point, growth, healing and happiness stop. Happiness is the best revenge, because it is no revenge. It could not be happy if there was revenge. The best you can get out of revenge is a self-righteous glee. Hurting yourself to get back at others is actually a form of masochism. Revenge is fear under the guise of aggression, the fear to live your life and to be free. While happiness is the by-product of love, intimacy and joining, revenge is a form of attack which separates further and avoids the real issue.

Revenge is an extreme form of holding on. It is a continuation of the power struggle which led to the break-up to begin with. A lost relationship typically reflects the 'I'll hurt myself to get back at you', or victim-type revenge. This is based on frustrated needs rather than love. It is not only a revenge on your ex-partner, but probably on one or both of your parents for not loving you more, and probably also on God.

Psychologically, every interpersonal conflict reflects the conflict in your own mind. Revenge is like cutting off your nose to spite your face.

Exercise

Your revenge is not getting you what you want, just as your relationship did not give you what you wanted, or you would not have lost it, despite your conscious protests to the contrary. If you are in pain, you are getting revenge. Otherwise, there is simply poignancy, as you feel and let go of any feelings which aren't happy.

'Happiness is the best revenge, because it is no revenge.'

DAY 23
Letting go and your higher self

Letting go and your higher self

I am a Doctor of Psychology, a kind of artist-scientist of the human mind, with a leaning towards therapy. I have seen too much, in and out of therapeutic settings, to discount a Higher Power by whatever name you prefer to give It. There is also a power in the human mind which is capable of magic and miracles. I am dedicated to learning and utilising this part of our mind. Call it the Higher Power, the Creative Self, the Christ Self, the Buddha Self, the Higher Mind or the Holy Spirit, it will not be diminished. It is the part of your mind which has all of your answers, and is trying to make your life easy. If you do not believe any of this, you are left with psychology or even slower methods. The best way is always with 'grace'.

I have discovered a number of things in my two decades plus sojourn as an explorer of the human mind. One is that it is only difficult when you are trying to do it yourself. This is a common malady of independent people. Interdependent people work with others and with grace a great deal more. Not that there are not problems for everyone, but interdependent people quickly remember not to try to do everything themselves. People only do this when they are trying to prove something. Interdependent people are entwined in a healthy fashion with others and with the Higher Self. They are better at relationships and at receiving. Every attachment you let go of leads you more and more towards interdependence and re-connection or realisation of lost bonding. There is no pain which does not come from attachment, and there is no fear which is not a fear of loss. The more one is connected with the Higher Self, the more one lives a life of ease and of grace, knowing how much more satisfying and successful it is to be creative rather than attached.

The job of your Higher Mind is to solve problems for you, to give answers to you and to help you out of seemingly impossible situations. Mostly, we want to do it ourselves, using our everyday mind. This means we are, at least, in control, even if it is miserable. And it is worth it to have this control, isn't it? Well, *isn't it*?

The situation of letting go could be easy. You could put it in the hands of your Higher Self. Holding on is really only a way of hiding from yourself, which is to say from your *Self*. Who are you really? And what did you come here to accomplish? What was it you promised before you came here? What did you want to contribute? Holding on is a trap whose purpose is to keep you in delay as long as possible. And, if you waste time, time wastes you. Do not waste yourself any longer! It is not worth it. It is time to begin again. *Yes!*

Exercise

Place whoever it is you are letting go of in the hands of your Higher Self. You might visualise, feel or sense this letting go. You might make it a prayer, or just hear yourself saying the words. When this occurs, there is usually a sense of peace, or of a gift being given in return. Make it easy on yourself, give it to your Higher Self.

Now place your future in the hands of your Higher Self. Today, place any fear, care, worry, depression, guilt or bad feeling in the hands of your Higher Self.

'Holding on is really only a way of hiding from yourself, which is to say from your *Self.*'

DAY 24

Letting go of the bad, letting go of the good

Letting go of the bad,
letting go of the good

If you have been in a letting go situation before, you will probably recognise that you first let go the bad and then let go of what was good in the relationship. Primarily, you recognise you are holding on and caught up in what was painful about the relationship. You work on the problem, bad feeling and grievances. But, after a while, these seem to fall into perspective and they are no longer as pressing or painful. You have moved through the pain and somehow have resolved that which held you back. Now what comes up is something entirely different, unless the relationship was entirely negative. What you find yourself thinking about is all of the good things. And it usually is harder and takes longer to let go of what you loved. Maybe it is because we are so used to the bad things we seemingly always have to deal with in a relationship, that the good things seem harder to come by. In most relationships, it is the good which is held on to most tightly, long after the other partner has gone. Often, after a death, a partner idealises their late partner, almost raising them to sainthood. Sometimes, you can tell what stage of the letting go process you are in just by knowing whether you are working on letting go of the bad things of the relationship or on the good things.

While it is important to resolve and let go of the negative, so that a pattern is not created, it is also important to let go of the good, so that it can reappear again in relationships to come.

Exercise

First make a list of any bad feelings or situations about the relationship you are holding on to, if any.

Next make a list of the good things in every area you are still holding on to about your ex-partner.

Put these in the hands of your Higher Self to let go of (unless you have found another more effective or favourite method – in which case use it).

Choose to trust and move forward with a new and willing openness.

'... let go of the good
so that it can reappear
in relationships to
come.'

DAY 25

Smiling their smile –
the gift of the relationship!

Smiling their smile –
the gift of the relationship!

Every relationship which reaches its potential has one major gift for those who are a part of it. And there are also plenty of other gifts. Sometimes, what a person gave you is so sweet and so deep it changed your life for ever. The love they gave you made a difference for who you are as a person. Sometimes it just seems too hard to let them go, even though they have gone on. Yet, it is only when you fully let go that the final gift of the relationship is yours. Doing this empowers you with the ability to give others what they gave you. Paradoxically, as you let go of them, what they gave you fully becomes part of you. What this means on an experiential level is that the emptiness they filled by being there is now filled by your own beingness through your letting go. The gift they gave you is now yours, and the loneliness is gone. It is a part of them which was extended to you, and has now become a part of you. It was something you learned in receiving from them. Now you can give it and make the same difference in others' lives as was made in yours. Now you can experience the joy of giving as you enjoyed the delight of receiving. Sometimes, you will smile their smile out at the world, or see through their eyes, as you perceive the beauty of something. And, as this new range of life they gave you is given, you will feel them and the bond they have with you, no matter what the external relationship may look like. Everything will feel OK and will be fine. You will look out at life and you will happily smile their smile. You will feel the goodness and the warmth once again. Your appreciation will be natural. There is a flow which will come to both your lives as you experience the goodness they gave you, especially when you now give this gift yourself.

Exercise

Today, have the courage to let them go. Notice there are those around you who need this same gift as was given you. You can give it. You can make a difference in their lives. And as you do, both of you will be helped. You have the choice of being held back, or you can make a difference to those around you. Sometimes, it will be as big a difference as was made in your life. Do you want to help? If you do, you will naturally hear the cries for help. Is your withdrawal, your holding on, your pain, more important than helping another? To truly help another would help you both. Would you continue in this holding on, this indulgence, if you knew someone s life depended on your giving? What was given you can make all the difference to others if only you choose to give it yourself.

This is a leadership principle. Whenever you are in pain, there is someone in greater need. If you give through your pain, not only the other, but you, too, will be helped.

'... it is only when
you fully let go that the
final gift of the
relationship is yours.'

DAY 26
Role playing

Role playing

Role playing is a way of gaining understanding and thus release from need, pain and fear. It can be used efficaciously to create the benefits of moving forward. This can be done with anyone you have unfinished business with, since understanding brings with it the power to release.

The first aspect is to get a friend, or someone else, to help you out. This process can be done over the phone, but it is more effective in person. If this is not going to be done with someone else, you might find it useful to tape (audio or video) your exercise and experience.

Exercise

The first part begins with a closed-eyed process by yourself. Use the time period of when you had the biggest misunderstanding with the other person involved. Imagine you are them as they were back then. Feel what it feels like to have their body. Experience all the sensation of that. When this feels complete, imagine what it feels like to have their emotions. What is it they are feeling? Experience all the sensations of that. When this feels complete, sense what it is like to have their thought processes. What is it they are thinking about? What is it that is always on their mind? Experience the sensation of that. After you have completed this exercise, write down any insights you have about what it was like being them, and why they were the way they were.

The next section is where you once again become the other person and let your friend question you about anything you do not understand about what your ex-partner did or why. If you do not have someone to assist you with this exercise, you can do it yourself. But, first, and once again, get the feeling your ex-partner was feeling. If you are doing it yourself, ask what was going on with them for them to have been doing that which you did not understand before. Ask yourself how long they have been feeling the feelings they were feeling, and even where those feelings had their beginning.

Now, let your friend be your ex-partner. Having them hear, feel, see and sense the way life and the relationship was for them as your partner. Ask them to feel intuitively what your ex-partner was experiencing for them to have acted the way they did. The person assisting you is not just to act and talk as they did; they are to feel and describe what was going on – role-playing as the ex-partner – describing how they were feeling for them to have acted in the manner they did.

DAY 27
Doing your part

1

2

Doing your part

As best as I can tell from all of the minds I have examined, everyone has a purpose ... and one which only you can do and be. Metaphorically, you might say that this purpose is a promise you made about the difference you would make in both your family and the world. As you fulfil your purpose, you also fulfil yourself. As you know and become your own self, and evolve towards becoming you best or Higher Self, you become a channel for grace. This way of being is naturally successful, and invites and assists others also to succeed naturally.

Your letting go allows others caught in similar situations to have the grace to let go. Your release becomes a channel for grace. Your evolution clears a path for everyone around you to move forward. We are locked in a certain energetic configuration with the people closest to us. As one person in the configuration shifts forward, everyone else in the configuration is allowed to shift forward. Your letting go is one less lesson your children will have to learn the hard way. Otherwise, every unresolved lesson gets passed down to your children to learn the hard way. Learning major lessons is like clearing a mine field through which your children, and other loved ones, will have to pass. By doing your part and letting go, what is now a mine field for you, can be a playground for them.

Your letting go and moving forward in a timely fashion is your gift to the world. This means there is one less bit of pain and illusion to resonate with other pain. There will now be a bit more flow which will help everything unfold more naturally. Your letting go and moving forward removes one more trap of pain from the world and adds that same degree of understanding. Healing moves you towards happiness and the realisation of your wholeness. Holding on just moves you towards more pain and death. It takes courage to move forward. And, in moving forward, anything could happen, even good things.

Exercise

Today, every time you think of the future, see, feel and sense its brightness. This is a choice – a choice to change all of your thoughts of pain to feeling good. Especially use the time just before you fall asleep, and the time just after you have awakened, to choose a happy day. See the future as brightening, feel it as free, hear yourself talking as you do when you are your best self. Notice every thought of fear, loneliness, depression, grievance or any form of bad feeling. Since every thought we have helps create our reality, it is important we be responsible – not only for our behaviour and our feelings, but also for our thoughts as well. Every time you catch yourself in anything but a happy, abundant, loving thought, make a new choice. Choose, see and feel the results of your choice as vividly as possible. Your thoughts are the order blanks you send into your life for which comes to pass.

'Your letting go and
moving forward in a
timely fashion is your
gift to the world.'

DAY 28
Goal setting and trust

Goal setting and trust

One of the antidotes which relieves and releases holding on is goal setting. Setting goals for yourself takes away the pressure of expectations or demands on yourself. It also sets up a flow where holding on has kept one stuck. With goal setting, you set where you want to be in a year, in six months, in three months, in a week and even by tomorrow. You move towards this goal as best as you can. If you find you have not reached your goal, or you have missed it, then you just reset the goal. Where is it you want to be by tomorrow? What is it you want to be feeling by then? How do you want the world to look to you? What do you want others to see when they look at you? Would you like to be able to bless your ex-partner when you think of them instead of feeling the knife in your heart? When you can bless them, you are equally blessed and your life is moved forward.

Trust, one of the core healing principles, helps both goal settings and letting go. Trust is acknowledging the power of your mind. Your mind is such that its power has to back something, and you get to decide what it backs. Trust is consciously putting your energy behind something, knowing it will work to your benefit, no matter how it looks now. The power of your mind can go towards fear or distrust if that is the direction you turn it in or it can move towards trust and unfolding things directly or paradoxically to your benefit.

When you goal set, the power of your mind works with you to help you reach your goals easily. It could just take a few minutes, if you wish, of just concentrating, imagining and putting your energy behind the realisation of your goal. This means your visualising, or experiencing it, as if it is already accomplished. Similarly, in letting go, trust helps you easily to bear the moment of empty-handedness experienced just after you let go. But, just as nature abhors a vacuum, your empty hands are soon filled in a happy way. Trust in letting go. Trust in what is coming next. When you trust, good things happen. Trust is not naiveté which overlooks denial, it is that which actively supports positive unfolding through the power of your heart and mind.

Exercise

Today, set goals for the next year. Every day examine your goals, especially the one for the day at hand. Recognise to what level you have succeeded. Then, reset your goal for the next day. Bring your trust to your letting go and to your goal setting. Trust yourself. Trust your ex-partner, and trust any other significant players in your drama.

'Trust is consciously
putting your energy
behind something,
knowing that it will
work to your benefit,
no matter how it looks
now.'

DAY 29
The script assigned – rules for relationships

1

2

The script assigned –
rules for relationships

People live by rules, or recipes, for certain situations. These are rules we have made for ourselves and rules which were imposed on us. We live by rules unless we have reached a high enough awareness to turn our rules into principles. Rules are defences, decisions which have come out of painful situations. They are meant to keep us from being hurt. The only problem is that rules are meant to be broken. Psychologically, defences attract attack and bring about the very thing they are trying to prevent. Rules, which are static, have a way of subconsciously reinforcing the very thing they are trying to prevent. The unresolved pain under every rule begs to be let out. The bigger the rule, the more the pain hidden beneath it, and the bigger the pain which will be called towards it to reopen the defence and allow the unfinished business to finally be finished.

We get upset in relationships because the other has broken our rules. Many times we do not even communicate our rules but expect our partner to be a mind reader. 'If they loved us, they would know, they would do what we wanted, or they would not do what we didn't want ...' So what happened is that your ex-partner broke your rules and it hurt. Not only did it hurt, but in our scripts we assigned them the supporting actor or actress roles to our stardom. Even if they seem to be given a lion's portion of the plot, there is only one star here and, of course, that is us. We do this out of our fear of an equal partner, which is a fear of intimacy. Without healing this fear, we will never get past our rules and scripts into principles, partnership and co-creativity. Now is the time to finish the pain inside and turn those rules into principles.

Exercise

Make a list of the major rules you have for relationships, eg. fidelity, honesty, communication, etc. Ask yourself intuitively, when you made up this rule, with whom was it made and in what circumstances?

Ask your Higher Mind to carry you and everyone in the situation back to their centres, that place of peace and innocence, so you all might experience peace, wholeness and grace. From this place, give the people in the situation the gifts you have come to give them. As you give the gift, receive it also into your life. What principle now comes into your life? What does your script look and feel like now?

'Now is the time to
finish the pain inside
and turn those rules
into principles.'

DAY 30
What is it you want?

What is it you want?

This is a good time to examine what it is you really want from life. What is it you really want in a relationship? Probably, as these last thirty days have gone by, you have become more and more willing to move forward in your life. But what is it you wish to move towards? How do you want your life to turn out? Do you want your life to end here, stopped by this emotional hazard? Your only joy here on this earth is really to be happy, or to heal so we can be happy. Most of life is an attempt at doing things to make us happy. All the rest is what we are doing to prove that we are good people. Think of it. What is it you are always telling your friends about your life?

Usually this comes under three general categories: 1) how good it is! or 2) how bad/hard it is! or 3) how hard it was but I accomplished it. These are stories we have been telling for years. They usually put a slight, or not so slight, barrier between us and our audience, because we would tell this to any audience. We are not relating, we are telling our story. Good stories are compensations for feeling bad or guilty inside. Bad stories are how tough life is ... please love me (victim story). Or how hard/busy life is, but I have handled it (hero story). Or how rotten other people are and, of course, I am so good (victim story). All of which again hides how valueless we feel inside that we would punish ourselves or compensate through hard work for our bad feelings. All of these stories are part of our conspiracy against ourselves. We use them to hide who we are and to hide our major gifts.

What is it you want in your life? You are at a birthing point, a place for a new beginning, a new chapter. You can choose to live in a whole new way, and leap forward out of your present experience. You can choose a happy, peaceful story. It may be undramatic, but the love and creativity would more than satisfy the need for stimulation.

Exercise

Look at what your story is hiding. What is the gift hidden so well under your conspiracy against yourself and against your greatness? Remember the difficulty or problem tends to be opposite to what the gift is, thus keeping it well disguised. Once you have this gift in mind, use it when you think of your future. Nothing can go wrong with your life when you are employing your gift. Become aware you have no neutral thoughts. Your thoughts are either about love and success or against them. Every time you think a thought about the past or future which is not a happy thought, see and feel your gift added to this thought or situation. You will notice everything goes better with your gift. Today, share this gift in whatever way you feel inspired to with someone else. As you give it, feel yourself receiving it. You will naturally feel better and more confident about life!

'You can choose to live
in a whole new way,
and leap forward out of
your present
experience.'

Chuck Spezzano PhD. is a world-renowned counsellor, trainer, author, lecturer and visionary leader. He holds a Doctorate in Psychology. From 26 years of counselling experience and 23 years of psychological research and seminar leadership, Dr Spezzano and his wife, Lency, created the breakthrough therapeutic healing model PSYCHOLOGY OF VISION. The impact of this model has brought deep spiritual, emotional and material change to thousands of participants from around the world.

The PSYCHOLOGY OF VISION is a path of the heart which acts as a bridge between psychology and grace. It transcends religious and cultural differences by recognising the three key concepts of relationships, leadership and spirituality.

Psychology of Vision contact details:

HAWAII:
Spezzano & Associates Ltd
PO Box 1021, Kaneohe
Hawaii 96744-1021
USA
Tel: (808) 239 4502 Fax: (808) 239 5424 E-Mail: vision@aloha.net

UNITED KINGDOM:
Creative Leadership Ltd
Townsend
Poulshot
Devizes
Wiltshire SN10 1SD
Tel: (44) 01380 828394 Fax: (44) 01380 828671
E-Mail: 106417.3713@compuserve.com

CANADA:
True Light Enterprises
6540 East Hastings Street
Dept 331, Burnaby
BC. Canada V5B 4Z5
Tel: 604 298 4011 Fax: 604 298 6755 E-Mail: trulite@ibm.net

SWITZERLAND:
POV Schweiz
Postfach 7920
CH 3001 Bern
Switzerland
Tel: 41 31 972 5525 Fax: 41 31 972 5577 E-Mail: pov@access.ch

TAIWAN:
Spiritual Ocean International Institute
Suite 1905, 19/F No. 171 Song-Der Road
Taipei
Taiwan
Republic of China
Tel: 886 2 759 5366 Fax: 886 2 759 5059 E-Mail: spiocean@m15hinet.net

JAPAN:
Rama Creative Institute
2-3 Oisecyo
Nakagawaku
Nagoya
Japan
Tel: 81 52 353 8555 Fax: 81 52 353 8899 E-Mail: rama@alles.or.jp

Vision Dynamics Institute
Koike Building 3F
1-8-8 Higashi Azabu
Minato-Ku
Tokyo 106
Japan
Tel: 81 33588 1031 Fax: 81 33588 1805